Just a Thought

A Collection of Devotional Meditations For Personal and Public Worship

compiled by

Juanita E. Thomas

Scythe Publications, Inc.
A Division of Winston-Derek Publishers Group, Inc.

© 1996 by Juanita E. Thomas

All rights reserved. No part of this book may be reproduced in any form without written permission from the publishers, except by a reviewer who may quote brief passages in a review to be printed in a newspaper or magazine.

First printing

PUBLISHED BY SCYTHE PUBLICATIONS, INC.
A Division of Winston-Derek Publishers Group, Inc.
Nashville, Tennessee 37205

Library of Congress Catalog Card No: 93-61293
ISBN: 1-55523-582-1

Printed in the United States of America

This collection is dedicated to two beautiful young women,

my daughters Valda and Sonia.

I love you.

"Let the words of my mouth and the meditations of my heart be acceptable in thy sight, O Lord, my strength, and my redeemer."

Psalms 19:14 KJV

Contents

Part I
A Thought-a-Month   1

Part II
Devotions to Share   17

Part III
Collected Verse   33

Part IV
Thoughts for the Holidays   49

Part V
From the Seminar "Personal Devotions"   61

Part I

A Thought-a-Month

These meditations were first compiled when I was elected to serve as chaplain for the chapter in 1973, and they are dedicated to the women in the beautiful sisterhood of Delta Upsilon Omega Chapter, Alpha Kappa Alpha Sorority, Inc., Seattle, Washington.

The following pages contain inspiring thoughts that I used to open the sorority chapter meetings. Some thoughts are my own, some are favorites of mine borrowed from here and there, compiled for each of the twelve months. I have used them over and over and would like to pass them on.

Soror Juanita Ensley Thomas
Alpha Psi Chapter
Tennessee State University

January

"I have a dream." These are the famous words of one of America's greatest men. He dreamed of peace, brotherhood, understanding, and equal opportunity for all mankind.

As we begin the new year, I have a dream that America will wake up, wipe the scales from her eyes, and see the light of day. It is only natural to look back in retrospect, and at the same time look forward with perspective.

May we not lose faith in the country for which our hero died. Martin Luther King, Jr., once said that if a man is afraid to die for what he believes is right, then he is not worthy of living, and though he lives to reach the age of eighty, he died the moment he failed to live.

May our one resolution for this year be: We will resolve to live, to become involved, to sacrifice and even die for the cause for which we believe.

February

A Time of Love

What is love? It's a concern, a caring for the other person. So often we take love for granted, but this is the month to stop and say to a sister, a friend, a sweetheart, or a child: "I love you."

Three little words, oh how wonderful to hear, or to utter to someone dear. *I love you* means more than all you could ever do.

Like most things of importance, love takes time. Take time for love.

March

Think spring!

Which is the greater? The anticipation of the trip or the trip? For me it's the anxious hours before.

The Savior came so that we might have life and have it more abundantly, and springtime is a renewal of that abundant life.

So don't just fret and complain.
Don't just sit and stare at the dark clouds and the rain.
Get up—get out.
Buy yourself a new outfit—a new hat.
Plant some flowers.
Plant a garden.
Go for a walk—think spring!

April

Showers of Blessings

> There shall be showers of blessing,
> This is the promise of love.
> There shall be seasons refreshing
> Sent from the Savior above.

These lines from a famous old hymn should remind us to count our blessings, even the blessing of rain, and of the seasons.

Wouldn't life be boring if every day were the same? Stop, look, and count your blessings. Each day brings new joys, and yes, new sorrows, too. But remember, without the sorrows, we could not appreciate the joys.

May

It may be early for planting a garden, but this one is unique. You can plant this garden anytime. In fact, see to it that you do, even if you do not consider yourself to be a gardener. I think you will have good luck with it.

A Rare Garden

First plant five rows of "peas" (*P*'s): presence, promptness, preparation, perseverance, and personal sacrifice. Next to these plant three rows of "squash": squash gossip, squash criticism, and squash indifference.

Then plant five rows of "lettuce": let us be unselfish, let us be loyal, let us be true, let us obey rules, and let us love one another.

No garden is complete without "turnips": turn up at all meetings, turn up with a smile, turn up with new ideas, and turn up with determination to make everything count for something good and worthwhile.

Where will you plant this garden? Plant it in your daily living, in service to your church, and in working for small organizations and groups.

June

You have probably heard the story of the farmer that found a baby eagle, took it home, and put it among his chickens. As it grew among the chickens, it thought it was a chicken and scratched around for its food.

A naturalist came by one day and became very disturbed. He took the eagle and placed it on his arm and told it, "Thou are an eagle. Take to your wings and fly." It just hopped down and started scratching around with the chickens again. He then took the eagle to the roof of the house and told it again, "Thou art an eagle. Take to your wings and fly." The same thing happened as before. He then decided to take the eagle to the mountains, and on a high mountain slope he said once more, "Thou art an eagle. Take to your wings and fly." The eagle then lifted its powerful wings and flew, soaring high. It was never seen again amongst the chickens.

Let's all be eagles—that is the way God planned us to be.

Remember that triumph is just a little *umph* added to *try*!

July

Today

Today is ours; let's live it.
Love is strong; let's give it.
If a song can help; let's sing it!

Peace is priceless; let's keep it.
The past is done; let's forget it.
Our work is here; let's do it.

If the world is wrong; let's right it.
If the road is rough; let's clear it.
The future is vast; don't fear it!

If faith is asleep; let's wake it.
Today is ours; make the most of it!

—Anonymous

Being confident is this, that He who began a good work in you will carry it on to completion until the day of Christ Jesus.

—Philippians 1:6

August

The last chance at summer. In June, you had all the time in the world. Spring ended and summer began. The skies were blue, the air was clear and warm, and getting warmer all the time. Plans were made about how and what you would do with summertime. Then came July. It was hot; the days were long, and it seemed it would last forever.

But now it's August, and you must hasten to get those summer things done or you will have to wait until next year.

Benjamin Mays once said, "Not failure, but low aim is sin!"

So, teach us to number our days, that we may apply our hearts unto wisdom.

—Psalms 90:12

September

If Jesus Came to Your House

If Jesus came to your house to spend a day or two, if he came unexpectedly, I wonder what you'd do? Oh, I know you'd give him your nicest room, this honored guest. And all the food you'd serve him would be the very best. And you would keep assuring him you're glad to have him there, that serving him in your home is joy beyond compare.

But when you saw him coming, would you meet him at the door, with arms outstretched in welcome to your Heavenly visitor? Or would you have to change your clothes before you let him in? Or hide some magazines and put the Bible where they'd been? Would you turn off the television and hope he hadn't heard, and wish you hadn't uttered that loud, nasty word?

Would you hide your worldly music and put some hymn books out? Could you let Jesus walk right in or would you rush about? And I wonder if the Savior spent a day or two with you would you go right on saying the things you always say? Would life for you continue as it does from day to day?

Would your family conversation keep up its usual pace? And would you find it hard each meal to say a table grace? Would you sing the songs you always sing, and read the books you read? And let him know the things on which your mind and spirit feed? Would you take Jesus with you everywhere you planned to go? Or would you maybe change your plans for just a day or so?

Would you be glad to have him meet your closest friends, or would you hope they'd stay away 'til his visit ends? Would you be glad to have him stay forever on and on, or would you sigh with relief when he at last was gone? It might be interesting to know the things that you would do, if Jesus Christ in person came to spend some time with you.

—Anonymous

October

An Indian Prayer

O great spirit,
Whose voice I hear in the winds,
And whose breath gives life to all the world
Hear me! I am small and weak,
I need your strength
And wisdom.

Let
Me
Walk
In beauty,
And make my eyes
Ever behold the
Red and purple sunset.

Make
My hands
Respect the things you have made, and my ears
Sharp to hear your voice.
Make me wise, so that I may understand the things
You have taught my people.
Let me learn the lessons you have hidden
In every leaf and rock.
I seek strength, not to be greater than my brother,
But to fight my greatest enemy, myself.
Make me always ready to come to you with
Clean hands and straight eyes.
So when life fades, as the fading sunset,
My spirit may come to you
Without shame.

November

A time of thanks. The fields are white and ready to harvest, but the laborers are few.

This year we are told to driver slower, kill-a-watt, and reserve power, but amidst it all we can pause and give thanks for life, health, shelter, work, play, friends, obligations, dedications, joys, and sorrows.

The future is not ours to see, but for today we give thanks. We have twenty-four hours each to share, be a friend, or lend a helping hand. You and I must do what we can. We can give thanks.

Scripture: *Psalm 100:1–5*

Prayer

Dear Lord and father of mankind, make us thankful for all blessings be they great or small. You made the world and all that within it dwells. Thank you, Lord. Amen.

December

My Christmas Gift to You:
Three Little Words

Seek
PEACE

Show
LOVE

Reap
JOY

Part II

Devotions to Share

Thanksgiving

Come ye thankful people come
Raise the song of harvest home.
All are safely gathered in
Ere the winter storms begin.
God, our Maker, doth provide
For our wants to be supplied
Come to God's own temple, come
Raise the song of harvest home.

I am so grateful that Christ is in my life. What would my life be without Him? It would be very dark and grim. When I'm sad, He cheers me. When I'm lonely, He will my comfort be. That's why I'm grateful, truly grateful. I'm so grateful that Christ is in my life.

As we reflect on another Thanksgiving season, let us thank God, truly thank Him for more than just the turkey and all the fixings. Let us thank Him for more than the pumpkin and sweet potato pies and the cranberry sauce.

Let us rejoice with Paul as he reminded the folks in Macedonia to be eager to give, to help God's people. In II Corinthians 9, the people's enthusiasm to give causes Paul to boast.

"Yes, God will give you much so that you can give away much," Paul says, "and when we take your gifts to those who need them they will break out in thanksgiving and praise to God for your help."

A Thankful Heart

America has only 6 percent of the world's population, yet we are blessed with:
- 33 percent of the world's production
- 33 percent of the world's college students
- 49 percent of the world's telephones
- 50 percent of the world's air travel
- 60 percent of the world's automobiles

Television, running water, and electric washers and dryers are common even among the poorest people, while the average underprivileged countries struggle for their most basic food and shelter.

We have FREEDOM to learn,
and FREEDOM to earn;
We have FREEDOM to move,
and FREEDOM to improve;
We have FREEDOM to gather
or not, if we'd rather;
We have FREEDOM to believe,
to write, talk, give or receive.

We have the greatest freedom and the most of the world's goods. Here freedom and abundance counsel together.

What more can I ask?
Lord, Thou hast given me many things; now give me yet one more: *a thankful heart.*

Lord, Teach Us to Pray

If pains afflict, or wrongs oppress,
If cares distract, or fears dismay,
If quiet dejects, if sins distress
Tell God about it now, don't delay!

Scripture: *Matthew 6:5–13 (Living Bible)*

How to pray—

1. Pray where you are, if possible in a quiet place alone.
2. Pray to God simply and naturally, as talking to a friend.
3. Pray, thanking God for the good things he has done for you.
4. Pray for God's forgiveness.
5. Pray for your needs.
6. Pray for others.
7. Pray, above everything else, that God's will be done.
8. Pray expecting answers.

How to Pray with Scripture References—

Follow Jesus' teachings and examples of prayer:

>John 17:1–26
>Matthew 6:5–15
>Luke 11:1–13

Pray for:

Wisdom	James 1:5–8
Others	II Timothy 1:3–7
	James 5:13–16
Growing Love	Philippians 1:9–11

Experience in Faith

Out of World War II came many thrilling and exciting sagas of faith, but the one about Captain Eddie Rickenbacker and eight men on a rubber life raft on the Pacific is one to remember.

Their plane had been forced down and they were left drifting helplessly without food or water in the scorching tropic sun. All but one managed to survive for eight days on four small oranges— there was no other food, and no water. The heat, the hunger, and the exhaustion had brought them close to the breaking point.

Eddie Rickenbacker believed in prayer. He had been taught this from a child, and had been in life and death situations before. His men were young and needed the example of his great faith and trust. They had grown weary, and one had become violently ill from drinking seawater. Some were showing signs of delirium.

One of the men had a small Bible. It was suggested that the following passage, Matthew 6: 25–34, be read: "Therefore take no thought, saying What shall we eat? or, What shall we drink? or Wherewithal shall we be clothed? for your heavenly Father knoweth that we have need of these things . . . But seek ye first the kingdom of God, and His righteousness; and all these things shall be added unto you. Take therefore no thought for the morrow; for the morrow shall take thought for the things of itself. Sufficient unto the day is the evil thereof."

What happened next, they tell, seemed like a miracle to the suffering men, like a direct answer to their prayer. A gull flew in and they had food, and they ran into a rainstorm and they had water. Food and water! The experience filled the men with awe and astonishment, and now they all prayed with confidence, with strong new faith. From then on they believed with the Captain that God was with them and that they would be saved.

And they were! They drifted for nearly two weeks longer, but at last they were spotted and picked up by another plane. And when they told their story and tried to explain, it always came out the same—a simple, unaffected explanation: "We prayed."

Scripture: *Colossians 2:7 (Living Bible)*
Hymn: *Have Thine Own Way Lord*

All God's Children

Scripture: *Matthew 18:1–6, 10; Mark 10:13–16*

These words of Jesus provided a mandate for us as Christians as we observed the International Year of the Child.

The United Nations Children's Fund (UNICEF), established in 1946, was the agency designated to disseminate information and spearhead projects relating to the International Year of the Child 1979.

Just what led us to this declaration? We love our children, and we provide for them—or do we?

Statistics tell us that:

> One child of every six is living with only one parent.
> 28 percent of teenagers are problem drinkers.
> 266,000 children are in foster homes.
> One million children are affected by divorce.
> In 1976, 205,000 babies were born to unmarried girls ages 15–19.
> 175,000 were placed because of abuse, neglect, and exploitation.

It is impossible for individuals, single churches, or even a particular denomination to deal with these problems alone, but when we band together, join hands with fellow Christians, and utilize agencies that are equipped to do what we cannot do by ourselves, I believe we are fulfilling our biblical injunction.

Let us review the United Nations Declaration of the Rights of the Child. Every child is entitled to:

>Affection, love, and understanding.
>Adequate nutrition and medical care.
>Free education.
>Full opportunity for play and recreation.
>A name and nationality.
>Special care, if handicapped.
>Be among the first to receive relief in times of disaster.
>Be a useful member of society and develop individual abilities.
>Be brought up in a spirit of peace and universal brotherhood.
>Enjoy these rights, regardless of race, color, or sex.

>Jesus loves the little children,
>all the children of the world.
>Red, yellow, black and white.
>All are precious in His sight.

Touch Someone Today

Acceptance toward ourselves.
Understanding toward others.
Assurance toward God.

One writer has called these attitudes "the ABC's of spiritual dynamics. The person who has all three is a person ready for service and is destined to be used by God."

Still another writer says there are five essential steps into the fullness of life:

> To accept oneself
> To be oneself
> To forget oneself in loving
> To believe
> To belong

I would now like to elaborate on our first premise, A. U. A.

> *Acceptance* toward ourselves—To thine own self be true.

> *Understanding* toward others—Be humble, gentle, and patient, always show you love by being helpful to one another (Ephesians 4:2).

> *Assurance* toward God—Be very sure you know God. Then let your life touch someone today.

How Real is Your Faith in God?

Scripture: *James 1:5–7, 2:17–22*

In times like these, you need an anchor. This rock is Jesus, yes he's the one. Be very sure, be very sure your anchor holds and grips the solid Rock.

Father Abraham was probably one of our best examples of a man who put his faith on the line, so to speak. He was obedient to God's command. What person in his/her right mind would kill his own child? Today he would have been committed, thrown in jail for even the attempt. But then I hear Elisha Hoffman ask, "Is your all on the altar?"

You have longed for sweet peace, and for faith to increase,
And have earnestly and fervently prayed.
But you cannot have rest or be perfectly blest,
Until all on the altar is laid.

Would you walk with the Lord, in the light of His word,
And have peace and contentment always?
You must do His sweet will, to be free from all ill,
On the altar your all you must lay.

O we never can know what the Lord will bestow
Of the blessings for which we have prayed,
Till our body and soul He doth fully control,
And our all on the altar is laid.

Meeting God at Every Turn

James asks, "Is your life full of difficulties and temptation? Then be happy, for when the way is rough, your patience has a chance to grow. So let it grow and don't squirm out of your problems. For when your patience is finally in bloom, then you will be ready for anything, strong in character, full and complete."

Catherine Marshall was the wife of the late Peter Marshall, the famous pastor of the New York Avenue Presbyterian Church, chaplain of the United States Senate, and hero of his wife's first bestseller, *A Man Called Peter*.

Catherine Marshall shares in her book a doing, working faith. She met and married a young minister, bore one son, then became ill and for about two years was confined to bed with tuberculosis. Her husband died when she was about thirty-five, leaving her alone to raise a son. She had no means of supporting herself except through her writing. She stepped out on faith, and with God's help, she became one of the greatest inspirational writers of our day. She later remarried a man with three children and started life all over again, again in faith.

With Him all things are possible; only trust Him.

See James 1:5–8 (Living Bible)

Three Gardens

1. The Garden of Eden
    A. Planted by God Himself. Everything was lovely: a model garden, with peace, joy, love, and happiness (Genesis 1:31).
    B. Adam was the gardener, to prune and keep it lovely.
    C. Sin caused us to lose the garden.

In the Garden

I come to the garden alone,
While the dew is still on the roses;
And the voice I hear, falling on my ear,
The son of God discloses.

He speaks, and the sound of His voice
Is so sweet the birds hush their singing;
And the melody that He gave to me
Within my heart is ringing.

I'd stay in the garden with Him
Tho the night around be be falling;
But He bids me go thru the voice of woe,
His voice to me is calling.

Refrain:
And He walks with me, and He talks with me,
And He tells me I am His own,
And the joy we share as we tarry there,
None other has ever known.

—C. Austin Miles

2. The Garden of Gethsemane
    A. Sorrow, the betrayal (Matthew 26:26–41).
    B. Reflect, watch, and pray.
    C. Willing spirit, weak flesh.

Lest I Forget Gethsemane

King of my life I crown Thee now
Thine shall the glory be;
Lest I forget Thy thorn-crowned brow,
Lead me to Calvary.

Show me the tomb where Thou wast laid.
Tenderly mourned and wept;
Angels in robes of light arrayed
Guarded Thee whilst Thou slept.

Let me like Mary, thru the gloom,
Come with a gift to Thee;
Show to me now the empty tomb
Lead me to Calvary.

May I be willing, Lord, to bear
Daily my cross for Thee;
Even Thy cup of grief to share
Thou has borne all for me.

Chorus:
Lest I forget Gethsemane,
Lest I forget Thine agony,
Lest I forget Thy love for me,
Lead me to Calvary.

—William J. Kirkpatrick

3. The Garden of Prayer

    A. Plant it where you will (Psalm 2).
    B. Prune and care for it daily.
    C. A special meeting place.

The Beautiful Garden of Prayer

There's a garden where Jesus is waiting,
There's a place that is wondrously fair
For it glows with the light of His presence
'Tis the beautiful garden of prayer.

There's a garden where Jesus is waiting,
And I go, with my burden and care.
Just to learn from His lips words of comfort
In the beautiful garden of prayer.

There's a garden where Jesus is waiting,
And He bids you to come meet Him there,
Just to bow and receive a new blessing
In the beautiful garden of prayer.

Refrain:
O the beautiful garden, the garden of prayer,
O the beautiful garden of prayer!
There my Savior awaits, and He opens the gates
To the beautiful garden of prayer.

—*James H. Fillmore*

Part III

Collected Verse

Scripture Cake
(10-12 servings)

I Kings 4:22	3 1/2 cups sifted flour
I Corinthians 5:6	2 teaspoons baking powder
Leviticus 2:13	1/2 teaspoon salt
I Kings 10:10	1/4 teaspoon nutmeg
ibid.	1/4 teaspoon cinnamon
ibid.	1/4 teaspoon allspice
Judges 5:25	1 cup butter
Jeremiah 6:20	2 cups sugar
Isaiah 10:14	6 eggs
Genesis 24:17	1 cup water
Exodus 3:8	3 Tablespoons honey
I Samuel 30:12	2 cups raisins
ibid.	2 cups chopped figs
Genesis 43:11	1 cup chopped walnuts

Sift and blend flour, baking powder, salt, and spices. Cream butter and sugar; stir until fluffy. Stir in eggs. Sift in about 1/4 cup of flour mixture over mixture in bowl and mix well. Stir in about 1/3 cup of water; add remainder of flour and water alternately, stirring between each addition until smooth. Follow Solomon's advice for making good men out of growing boys (Proverbs 23:13) and beat well by hand at least 8–10 minutes. Add honey, raisins, chopped figs, and walnuts. Stir until well mixed. Pour into 10-inch greased tube pan and bake at 350° F. for about 90 minutes, until toothpick inserted near center comes out clean.

Slow Me Down, Lord

Slow me down, Lord!
Ease the pounding of my heart
By the quieting of my mind.
Steady my harried pace
With a vision of the eternal reach of time.
Give me,
Admidst the confusions of my day,
The calmness of the everlasting hills.
Break the tensions of my nerves
With the soothing music of the sighing streams
That live in my memory.
Help me to know
The magical restoring power of sleep.
Teach me the art
Of taking minute vacations; of slowing down to look at
a flower;
To chat with an old friend or make a new one;
To pat a stray dog;
To watch a spider build a web;
To smile at a child;
Or to read a few lines from a good book.
Remind me each day
That the race is not always to the swift;
That there is more to life than increasing its speed.
Let me look upward
Into the branches of the towering oak
And know that it grew slowly and well.
Slow me down, Lord,
And inspire me to send my roots deep
Into the soil of life's enduring values
That I may grow toward the stars
Of my greater destiny.

—*Wilferd A. Peterson*

Four Kinds of Bones

There are *wishbones* who spend their time wishing somebody else
would do the work.
And then there are the *jawbones* who do all the talking
but very little else.
Next come the *knucklebones*, who knock everything
that everybody else tries to do.
And finally there are the *backbones* who get under the load
and do all the work.
Which are you?

Which Member Are You?

Are you an active member,
        The kind that would be missed?
Or are you just contented,
        That your name is on the list?

Do you attend the meeting
        And mingle with the flock?
Or do you stay at home
        To criticize and knock?

Do you take an active part
        To help the work along?
Or are you satisfied to be
        Among the kinds that just belong?

Do you ever visit
        A member that is sick?
Or leave the work to just a few
        And talk about the clique?

Think this over, member,
        You know right from wrong—
Are you an active member,
        Or do you just belong?

I Shall Not Pass This Way Again

Through this toilsome world, alas!
Once and only once I pass;
If a kindness I may show,
If a good deed I may do
To a suffering fellow man,
Let me do it while I can.
No delay, for is is plain
I shall not pass this way again.

—*Author unknown*

The Lord Is My Shepherd

The Lord is my shepherd; I shall not want.
    He maketh me to lie down in green pastures:
    He leadeth me beside the still waters.

He restoreth my soul:
    He leadeth me in the paths of righteousness
    for His name's sake.

Yea, though I walk through the valley of the
    shadow of death, I will fear no evil:
    for thou are with me;
    thy rod and they staff they comfort me.

Thou preparest a table before me
    in the presence of mine enemies:
    thou anointest my head with oil;
    my cup runneth over.

Surely goodness and mercy shall follow me
    all the days of my life: and I will
    dwell in the house of the Lord forever.

—Psalm 23 KJV

The King of Glory

The earth is the Lord's, and the fullness thereof; the world, and they that dwell therein.

For he hath faith founded it upon the seas, and established it upon the floods.

Who shall ascend into the hill of the Lord? or shall stand in his holy place?

He that hath clean hands, and a pure heart; who hath not lifted up his soul unto vanity, nor sworn deceitfully.

He shall receive the blessing from the Lord and righteousness from the God of his salvation.

This is the generation of them that seek him, that seek thy face, O Jacob. Selah.

Lift up your heads, O ye gates; and be ye lift up, ye everlasting doors; and the King of glory shall come in.

Who is this King of glory? The Lord strong and mighty, the Lord mighty in battle.

Lift up your heads, O ye gates; even lift them up, ye everlasting doors; and the King of glory shall come in.

Who is this King of glory? The Lord of hosts, he is the King of glory. Selah.

—Psalm 24 KJV

Open My Eyes, That I May See

Open my eyes, that I may see
Glimpses of truth Thou hast for me;
Place in my hands the wonderful key
That shall unclasp, and set me free.

Open my ears, that I may hear
Voices of truth Thou sendest clear;
And while the wave-notes fall on my ear,
Everything false will disappear.

Open my mouth, and let me bear
Gladly the warm truth everywhere;
Open my heart, and let me prepare
Love with Thy children thus to share.

Refrain:
Silently now I wait for Thee,
Ready, my God, Thy will to see;
Open my eyes, illumine me, Spirit divine!
Open my ears, illumine me, Spirit divine!
Open my heart, illumine me, Spirit divine!

—*Clara H. Scott*

Prayer of St. Francis of Assisi

Lord, make me an instrument of Thy peace;
where there is hatred, let me sow love;
where there is injury, pardon;
where there is doubt, faith;
where there is despair, hope;
where there is darkness, light;
and where there is sadness, joy.

O Divine Master, grant that I may not so much seek
to be consoled as to console;
to be understood, as to understand;
to be loved, as to love;
for it is in pardoning that we are pardoned,
and it is in dying
that we are born to eternal life.

The Pause that Refreshes
or Punctuation Marks of Life

The comma **,** a brief rest, the pause that refreshes.

The colon **:** the pause that translates.

The semicolon **;** the pause the renews.

The question mark **?** the pause that affirms.

The parentheses **( )** the pause that identifies.

The quotation marks **" "** the pause that remembers.

The period **.** the pause that terminates.

Prayer: Teach us, Dear Lord, to punctuate our days that we may apply them unto wisdom.

The Greatest Love

I may be able to speak the languages of men and even of angels, but if I have no love, my speech is no more than a noisy gong or a clanging bell. I may have the gift of inspired preaching; I may have all knowledge and understand all secrets; I may have all the faith needed to move mountains—but if I have no love, I am nothing. I may give away everything I have, and even give up my body to be burned—but if I have no love, this does me no good.

Love is patient and kind; it is not jealous or conceited or proud; love is not ill-mannered or selfish or irritable; love does not keep a record of wrongs; love is not happy with evil, but is happy with the truth. Love never gives up; and its faith, hope, and patience never fail.

Love is eternal. There are inspired messages, but they are temporary; there are gifts of speaking in strange tongues, but they will cease; there is knowledge, but it will pass. For our gifts of knowledge and of inspired messages are only partial; but when what is perfect comes, then what is partial will disappear.

When I was a child, my speech, feelings, and thinking were all those of a child; now that I am a man, I have no more use for childish ways. What we see now is like a dim image in a mirror; then we shall see face-to-face. What I know now is only partial; then it will be complete—as complete as God's knowledge of me.

Meanwhile these three remain: faith, hope, and love; and the greatest of these is love.

—*I Corinthians 13*

Joy in the Morning

Inspirational writings by Juanita E. Thomas
Compiled June 1986

My First Poem

I wrote my first poem today.

I liked the way it went.

I rather enjoyed the free flow of
thought and pen.

And maybe someday I'll even write again.

On the By-ways

On the by-ways of life, people come and people go.

It's interesting as I stand and watch as they go to and fro.

Some are rich and some are poor, some well dressed and some shabby, but they all have someplace to go.

I stand and watch as they parade by.

Up the street, down the street, some in a hurry and some a little slow.

Both the old and the young.

As the weather changes, they change too, and yet not really—

Because whatever the weather, whether hot or cold, they still go to and fro.

The Mountains are Mine

The mountains are mine
Oh how wonderfully blessed.
They are tall and short
and differently dressed.

Some are round and smooth
Some are jagged and rough
Some are pointed and
some are low
really only hills.

But they are beautifully attired
Some in gray,
Some in red clay,
Some in green because of the grass and
some are naked and
seem to lack class.

But they were made by God above
and he gave them in love
to help form the valleys
and an animal abode.

And because he made them,
I am his and he is mine,
then the mountains too are mine.

At the Foot of the Mountain

At the foot of the mountain
I sit and wait,
I wait for the master to open the gate,
The gate to restoration and light.

At the foot of the mountain,
the pasture is green.
I am refreshed and every
soul is swept clean.

At the foot of the mountain,
where all the cattle graze
He restoreth my soul and I give
him praise.

At the foot of the mountain
I can look up and behold
the lofty peaks reaching to the heaven
to have the story retold.

At the foot of the mountain,
the valley is peaceful.
Because Jesus died, my sins are all forgiven
because he arose, because he lives
I'm on my way to heaven.

Part IV

Thoughts for the Holidays

New Year's Day
January 1

A Lakota Indian Prayer

My spirit is one with You,
      Great Spirit.

You strengthen me day and
      night to share my very best
      with my brothers and sisters.

You, whom my people see in
      all of creation and in all
      people, show Your Love for us.

Help me to know, like the
      soaring eagle, the heights of
      knowledge.

From the Four Directions, fill
      me with the four virtues of
      Fortitude, Generosity,
      Respect and Wisdom;
      so that I will help my people
      walk in the path of
      Understanding and Peace.
      Amen.

St. Valentine's Day

February 14

Cupid was the God of Love. May the arrow that he brings pierce the heart of love and may this love be spread abroad 365 days of the year. May LOVE be more of an active verb than a proper noun.

So on this Valentine's Day symbolized by the red and white,
>Will you be my Valentine?
>Will you be my Valentine?
>Will you be my Valentine?

For God so loved the world that He gave His one and only son.
—John 3:16

Easter Sunday

or

Resurrection Sunday

Although Easter Sunday is defined as an annual Christian festival celebrating the resurrection of Jesus, some have discontinued the term *Easter* because of its origin or pagan connotation.

In the Christian church, the focus is on Jesus. Because of Good Friday, we have Resurrection Day. Jesus came and dwelt among the people, was crucified—on Friday, buried, and rose on the third day.

The new testament records the story of the resurrection at least three times. John 20:1–18 KJV, verification that *He lives!*

Mother's Day

Second Sunday in May

An old proverb says: "The hand that rocks the cradle rules the world." My father, a very wise man, who at the age of ninety-three can still recite gems of wisdom, would say that this is "more truth than poetry."

If the nation is to be saved, we must take back the home. Motherhood is sacred. Because of her, new life is developed, nurtured and produced. God instituted the family; he gave each member a definite role to play. How did we manage to get so far off track?

"Honor thy father and thy mother: that thy day may be long upon the land which the Lord thy God giveth thee."
—*Exodus 20:12 KJV*

Dear Lord, restore the sacred bond of motherhood and your divine plan of procreation. Amen.

Children's Day

Second Sunday in June

Children, obey your parents in the Lord, for this is right. Honor your father and mother—which is the first commandment with a promise—that it may go well with you and that you may enjoy life on earth.

—Ephesians 6:1–3

Father's Day

Third Sunday in June

Father's Day came later in our national celebrating than Mother's Day, but it is of no less importance. According to Genesis 1:27–28 KJV, "God created man in his own image, in the image of God created he him; male and female created he them. And God blessed them, and God said unto them, be fruitful, and multiply, and replenish the earth and subdue it."

The biological process has not changed, therefore father's role is most important. We must restore the sacredness of the home, family, and fatherhood.

"Honor thy father and mother; which is the first commandment with promise; That it may be well with thee, and thou mayest live long on the earth. And, ye fathers, provoke not your children to wrath; but bring them up in the nurture and admonition of the Lord.

—Ephesians 6:2–4

Dear Lord, restore the sacred bond of fatherhood and your divine plan of procreation. Amen.

Labor Day

If God Should Go on Strike

How good it is that God above
has never gone on strike,
Because He was not treated fair
In things He didn't like.
If only once, He'd given up
And said, "That's it, I'm through!
I've had enough of those on Earth,
So this is what I'll do:
I'll give my orders to the sun
Cut off the heat supply!
And to the moon give no more light.
And run the oceans dry.
Then just to make things really tough
And put the pressure on,
Turn off the vital oxygen
Till every breath is gone!"
You know He would be justified
If fairness was the game,
For no one has been more abused
Or met with more disdain
Than God, and yet He carries on
Supplying you and me
With all the favors of His grace.
And everything for free.
Men say they want a better deal,
And so on strike they go.
But what a deal we've given God
To whom all things we owe.
We don't care whom we hurt
To gain the things we like;
But what a mess we'd all be in
If God should go on strike.

A Thanksgiving Meditation

Divine Worship

Make a joyful noise unto the Lord, all ye lands.

Serve the Lord with gladness; come before his presence with singing.

Know ye that the Lord he is God; it is he that hath made us, and not we ourselves; we are his people, and the sheep of his pasture.

Enter into his gates with thanksgiving, and into his courts with praise; be thankful unto him, and bless his name.

For the Lord is good; his mercy everlasting; and his truth endureth to all generations

—*Psalm 100 KJV*

Every day should be a day of thanksgiving!

The Joy of Christmas

May Christmas Joy be ours this day,
Each praising God in His own way.
Regardless of sorry, death or war,
Remember the story of the star,
Yon angel choir with its song of peace.

Could we not yet hope that wars will cease?
Happiness come to everyone?
Recall the words of God's own Son,
In this shall all men know you are mine,
Showing to others God's love divine,
To all men of the human race
May they be white, or brown, or black of face
All that He asks is that we love—
So the real joy of Christmas prove.

Part V

From the Seminar "Personal Devotions"

Personal Devotions Seminar

Theme: He Lives; The Christian Way of Life

Goal/Purpose: The ready will to perform what belongs to the service of God. Religious observance or worship; a form of prayer or worship for special use.

Reference Material:

1. The Holy Bible (King James Version)

2. The Living Bible

3. Good New for Modern Man—New Testament

4. *The Secret Place*—quarterly, American Baptist Publication

5. *Light from Many Lamps*
   Lillian E. Watson, 1951

6. *Apples of Gold*
   Jo Petty, 1962

7. *Lord Could You Make It A Little Better?*
   Robert A. Raines, 1972

8. *Who Am I God?*
   Marjorie Holmes, 1973

9. *Martin Luther's Table Talk*
   Edited by David L. Scheidt, 1969

10. *Strength for Service*
    Arthur Sterling Ward, 1942

Lead Questions

1. Why the need for personal devotions?

2. Can devotions be just a prayer?

3. How do I get started?

4. How do I find the time?

5. Must I have this time every day?

6. But what if I can't word a prayer?

7. What if I don't know the books of the Bible?

8. What will my family think if I tell them not to disturb me for ten minutes each morning?

9. Can I use songs/hymns?

10. Can I start anytime?

Sweep over my soul, Sweep over my soul:
Come, gracious Spirit, Sweep over my soul
Sweep out hate and fear, Sweep out hate and fear;
Come, gracious Spirit; Sweep out hate and fear
Sweep in love and peace, Sweep in love and peace
Come, gracious Spirit, Sweep in love and peace.

Music

Music is one of the best art forms. We read in the Bible that the good and godly kings maintained and paid singers. Music is the best solace for a sad and sorrowful mind; it refreshes the heart and gives it a certain peace and calm. A means of communication is through the words and message of the hymns of the church.

I Must Tell Jesus

I must tell Jesus all of my trials;
I cannot bear these burdens alone;
In my distress He kindly will help me;
He ever loves and cares for his own.

I must tell Jesus all of my troubles;
He is a kind, compassionate Friend;
If I but ask Him, He will deliver,
Make of my troubles quickly an end.

Chorus:
I must tell Jesus! I must tell Jesus!
I cannot bear these burdens alone;
I must tell Jesus! I must tell Jesus!
Jesus can help me, Jesus alone.

He Lives

I serve a risen Savior, He's in the world today;
I know that He is living, whatever men may say;
I see His hand of mercy, I hear His voice of cheer,
And just the time I need Him, He's always near.

In all the world around me, I see His loving care,
And tho' my heart grows weary, I never will despair;
I know that He is leading thru all the stormy blast,
The day of His appearing will come at last.

Rejoice, rejoice, O Christian, lift up your voice and sing
Eternal hallelujahs to Jesus Christ the King!
The hope of all who seek Him, the Help of all who find,
None other is so loving, so good and kind.

Chorus:
He lives, He lives, Christ Jesus lives today!
He walks with me and talks with me along life's narrow way.
He lives, He lives, salvation to impart!
You ask me how I know He lives? He lives within my heart.

Is Your All on the Altar

You have longed for sweet peace, and for faith to increase,
And have earnestly and fervently prayed.
But you cannot have rest or be perfectly blest,
Until all on the altar is laid.

Would you walk with the Lord, in the light of His word,
And have peace and contentment always?
You must do His sweet will, to be free from all ill,
On the altar your all you must lay.

O we never can know what the Lord will bestow
Of the blessings for which we have prayed,
Till our body and soul He doth fully control,
And our all on the altar is laid.

Who can tell all the love He will send from above,
And how happy our hearts will be made,
Of the fellowship sweet we shall share at His feet,
When our all on the altar is laid.

Chorus:
Is your all on the altar of sacrifice laid?
Your heart, does the Spirit control:
You can only be blest and have peace and sweet rest,
As you yield to Him your body and soul.

Precious Lord

When my way is drear, Precious Lord linger near;
When my life is almost gone,
Hear my cry, hear my call, hold my hand lest I fall,
Take my hand, Precious Lord, lead me on.

When the darkness appear, and the night draws near,
And the day is past and gone,
At the river I stand, guide my feet, hold my hand—
Take my hand, Precious Lord, lead me on.

Chorus:
Precious Lord, hold my hand, lead me on, let me stand;
I am tired, I am weak, I am worn,
Through the storm, through the night,
Lead me on to the light,
Take my hand, Precious Lord, lead me on.

Inspiration

Take Time

> To Think: it is the source of power.
>
> To Play: it is the secret of perpetual youth.
>
> To Read: it is the fountain of wisdom.
>
> To Pray: it is the greatest power on earth.
>
> To Love and Be Loved: it is a God-given privilege.
>
> To Be Friendly: it is the road to happiness.
>
> —*Author Unknown*

Scripture References on Prayer

Will I pray . . . . Psalm 55: 17
and pray for them . . . . Matthew 5:44
pray to the Father . . . . Matthew 6:6
After this manner therefore pray . . . . Matthew 6:8
Watch and pray . . . . Matthew 26:41
Lord, teach us to pray . . . . Luke 11:1
always to pray . . . . Luke 18: 1
I will pray . . . . John 14:16
we should pray . . . . Romans 8:26
Pray without ceasing . . . . I Thessalonians 5:17
afflicted? let him pray . . . . James 5:13
and pray one for another . . . . James 5:16

Sixty Minutes of Prayer

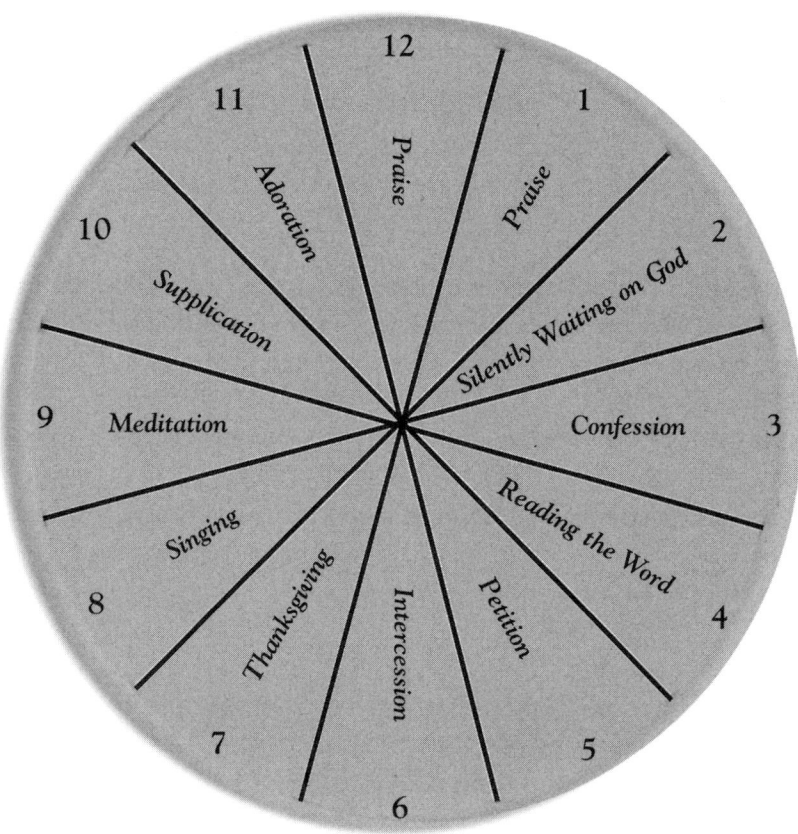

Confession—acknowledgement of sin in self.
Intercession—pray for others.
Petition—asking God to meet personal desires.
Praise—thanking God for creation.
Thanksgiving—to offer thanks to God for being good to us.
Meditation—thinking with mind and spirit about God.
Adoration—showing outwardly the soul's inward respect for God (bowing, kneeling, raising hands).
Supplication—humbly seeking forgiveness.

Scripture

Christianity is a full-time job; if we would be Christlike, we must work at at. We must study the word, seek God's will. The scriptures are a source of strength, and prayer a source of power.

In all fields of knowledge, the ablest professors are those who have thoroughly mastered the textbooks. In order to be a good lawyer, a man should have every text of the law at his fingertips. In Luke 8, Christ says, "Unto you it is given to know the mysteries of the kingdom of God."

When we seek after God, we shall find him in the midst of those who keep his word. Christ says: "If a man loves me, he will keep my words, and my Father will love him, and we will come unto him and make our abode with him." II Timothy 15 says, "Work hard so God can say to you, 'well done.' " Be a good workman, one who does not need to be ashamed when God examines your work. Know what His word says and means.

Prayer

No one can believe how powerful prayer is and what it is able to affect except those who have learned it by experience. Another word for prayer might be communication. Tell God what's on your mind. Express your desires, fears, joys, gratitude; tell Him all. You learn to pray by praying. The Lord's Prayer is our example, and a beautiful one it is: Matthew 6:9–13.

Ecclesiastes says, "The prayer of a good and godly Christian availeth more to health, then the physician's physic." O how great a thing, how marvelous, a godly Christian's prayer is. How powerful prayer is.

Seven Parts to Prayer

1. Adoration . . . . Psalm 18:1–2
2. Confession . . . . James 5:16, I John 1:8
3. Supplication . . . . Luke 18:3
4. Intercession . . . . Isaiah 53:12, Romans 8:26
5. Thanksgiving . . . . Ephesians 1:3, I Peter 1:3
6. Dedication . . . . Isaiah 26:13
7. Doxology . . . . I Timothy 1:17, Romans 16:27